Building a world class team:

Lessons from the FIFA World Cup 2010.

Copyright © 2012 by George Daoud

Table of Contents

Introduction 4

Part One 6

    Brief overview of the World Cup competition 8

Part Two 14

    France 16

    Italy 18

    England 21

    United States Of America 24

    Brazil 27

    Argentina 29

    Ghana 32

    Uruguay 35

    Germany 37

    Holland 41

    Spain 44

Conclusion 47

About the Author 50

Dedication

I dedicate this book to my wife Katrina, who's not a big fan of sports but always helps me and supports me.

Introduction

If someone told me one day I would write a book about team building and success, I might have laughed.

I am a technical 'computer guy' who likes to write source code and software. I never thought I would write a non-technical book until now.

You are probably wondering why I wrote this book. The topic hit me after a conversation with a friend while we were analyzing the team work, coordination and reasons for the failure or success of the teams in the tournament when I realized those same reasons apply to any team in any kind of business.

The second I began writing, it took over all my thoughts. I found myself constantly thinking about it and finding more interesting points. I finally decided to share my observations with anyone who might find them interesting and not only the people at work, which led me to this book.

Although I wrote about the reasons that made teams succeed or fail in the World Cup, my focus was not on the sport, the tournament or the games, but on team work, strengths and mistakes and how they apply to any job that requires a successful team.

Part One

The idea for this book started after watching the FIFA World Cup 2010, which occurred in June and July of 2010. Even if you do not follow the World Cup or like soccer, football or international football, this book is not about the game itself but examines the reasons some teams are successful and others fail in any business by analyzing the most popular sports tournament in the world.

My favorite football team is Brazil. I like the way they play, the team and the individual skills they have but in this World Cup, they lost against Holland and were removed from the tournament.

I was talking to one of my football friends and he said, "We (Brazil) lost everything because of one player." As he was telling me why he thinks so, I realized he was partially right. I believe there are other reasons why Brazil lost as well and this conversation opened my eyes to other things and made me curious about the performance of other teams in the tournament.

I started going over the different teams, trying to figure out why each succeeded or failed. I found this very interesting and I think you will too, after you read this book. I realized this also applies to my work or any work that has a team, so I started writing some notes about each team and decided to share it with my friends and write this book.

I do not want to write another typical team-building book, so I will show the key features for the successes and failures of a team based on real life experience from the largest sporting event in the world to give a better idea about the challenges that face a team while keeping the topic fun.

The reason I chose the 2010 FIFA world cup over other world cup occurrences is because this world cup in particular was special. The 2010 World Cup was held in Africa for the first time, so the home advantage was not in favor of the usual European or South American teams. Also this world cup witnessed a final between two teams that never won the world cup before. It included new emerging teams, several surprises and covered every reason that causes a team to fail or succeed. It was the perfect event for my book.

I believe what opened my eyes to the main team requirements discussed in this book started when I switched from startup and small businesses to a large-scale enterprise corporation. Challenges become increasingly difficult as the team size increases or the goal of the team becomes more difficult to achieve. This does not mean the points discussed in this book apply only to large teams, but they are more frequent and apparent in larger teams.

I hope you will find this book interesting and helpful in applying this positive information to avoid the pitfalls some of the teams in the World Cup fell into.

Brief overview of the World Cup competition

I promise not to bore you with the rules of the FIFA World Cup football competition, but if you are interested, you can find them at the FIFA web site, http://www.fifa.com.

My goal is to show you the magnitude and importance of this tournament for all the teams and players, in order to understand what they go through and what it means for a player to win the World Cup.

If you currently have a job, pause for one second and ask yourself this question, "What is the ultimate, highest accomplishment I can achieve in my current carrier path? Is it becoming a CEO or the owner of the company I work for or possibly a large salary increase so I can retire early?"

It does not matter what your ultimate goal might be. The most important thing is to have a goal and follow it. If you cannot think of one, I recommend you start defining a main goal now and follow it. You will have much better motivation when you have a goal.

For any football player, winning the World Cup is a once in a lifetime opportunity to shine and become part of history. It is the ultimate accomplishment they can achieve, and in order to do this, they have to face seven extremely difficult challenges, which I will describe below.

First Challenge: Get Selected to Play in the National Team.

FIFA has two hundred and eight members, three more than the International Olympic Committee. This is a total of two hundred and eight countries, which makes it larger than the United Nations.

Each country has thousands of football players and some countries, like Brazil, have more than half a million registered, professional players. Can you imagine the level of competency necessary to pick twenty-two players out of half a million to represent the country?

The players do everything they can to be selected by the national coach. For them this is the first big challenge to face.

Once the twenty-two players are selected, the coach has to determine the first eleven starters and their replacements, so within the national team, the players have to excel to be selected as a starter. No one wants to sit on the bench and watch the game.

Second Challenge: Consistency.

After the selection of the team, the training begins along with playing friendly games to test the harmony between players and assess their individual skills. If a player's performance starts decreasing or proves to be inconsistent, there is a chance the player will be replaced.

This fear of replacement can happen at any time, even while playing the qualifying games, so each player has to stay on top of his form.

The second big challenge for the players is to consistently maintain a competitive and strong performance in order to keep their chances high to play in the World Cup.

Maintaining a great performance requires not only the ability to play and train well, but also to avoid injuries and physical or mental damages. Many players lose their chance to join the World Cup only a few days before the event starts due to an injury. Others let their personal lives affect their performance.

This is important to remember. I never used to give it enough credit. In my job, I always thought I need to keep my technical skills up to date to remain on top of my duties, but I failed to realize that maintaining good health, morale and less stress is as important as the technical side. It is amazing how much health, stress and personal issues can affect the performance of the best expert in any field.

Third challenge: Qualification to the World Cup.

There are only thirty-two out of two hundred and eight teams that can make it to the World Cup. FIFA assembles teams of the same continent into different groups, and each team plays against all the other teams in their group. The top two teams from each group will be chosen to go to the World Cup.

FIFA selects five countries from Africa, four and a half from Asia, four and a half from South America, thirteen from Europe, three and a half from North and Central America and half a country from Oceania. I am sure you are wondering how they can pick half a team, but this means the seat is split between two continents and one team will pick the full seat after a decisive game.

Forth Challenge: Marketing

For the players, the World Cup is like attending a job interview. Most of the largest club owners and coaches from all over the world will be watching the games and taking notes of each player's performance, trying to decide who to hire for their club.

As a player, you need to outperform the other players competing in your position to convince these owners and coaches to choose you.

The World Cup is only one month out of every four years, so the player needs a full time job during these four years to make money, improve skills and impress the national team coach to pick him to play in the World Cup.

It is a dream come true for each player to play in the top clubs in the world such as Barcelona, A.C. Milan, Real Madrid, Manchester United and more. These clubs pay large amounts of money and get a lot of attention - they are very good for marketing purposes - and they have very competitive players to learn from. A good football player does not want to be chosen by just any small club because it might damage his career, but getting picked by these top clubs is not an easy job either.

Fifth Challenge: Reputation and image.
No player wants to be the reason his team loses. The player has to go back home and face his friends, neighbors and family. It will be embarrassing and difficult to return with a loss due to bad performance, or even worse, the player's own mistakes.

All these people put their faith and trust in the players and they will feel betrayed if the player does not put on a decent show. There are many times when the players who caused their team to lose had to return home and avoid facing people. This situation affects the morale of some players, and is one of the things they fear most.

Sixth Challenge: Winning the World Cup
This is the ultimate goal, but considering they will be facing the top thirty-one teams in the world and the best of the best, it is not a walk in the park.

This is more difficult than qualifying, especially that after the second round. One loss and they are out. The level of stress is enormous. Each player is afraid to be the one who makes the mistake that costs the whole team the tournament.

Seventh Challenge: Best Player Award.
This is more of a personal challenge. The FIFA selects the top scorer and the best player awards at the end

of the tournament. For many players, this is a dream to win. Can you imagine winning the best player award after facing the top best players in the world?

If you consider the seven challenges above and add four years of hard work to build a team and qualify, you can understand how stressful and 'scary' this tournament is for the players. One mistake and their whole carrier might be in jeopardy.

The World Cup is a once in a lifetime opportunity for many players. The reason is that not all of them join the national team very young. It takes time to build the skills and expertise that will enable a player to join the national selection, and the maximum age to play in the World Cup is thirty-four years old. This is not an official rule, but due to the amount of stamina and strength required, it would be nearly impossible for an older man to perform against the younger players. Many injuries also occur and there is no guarantee the player will be in good health when the next World Cup takes place.

Finally, keeping consistent performance and the ability to outperform all the new players in the nation who might surface during the next four years is not a guarantee. For all these reasons, smart players consider their participation in the World Cup as a one-time opportunity they need to seize.

Part Two

Now that you have a good idea about the World Cup, I would like to share with you the analysis of the reasons leading to the success or failure of the teams that participated in the 2010 World Cup. I will begin with the teams based on the order in which they left the tournament.

Although there are thirty-two teams in the tournament, I am only covering the teams that were likely candidates to win the World Cup before it started, or the teams that were not strong candidates but made it farther than expected, due to their fighting spirit and strong team players.

Several of the occasional teams are just happy to make it to the World Cup. This by itself is a big achievement for them. Some will show a fair performance and others a very poor performance because they seem satisfied that they made it this far and they strongly believe they cannot win, so they lack the motivation.

I believe it is bad if a team makes it all the way to the World Cup without trying their best to go further. I am sure some of the teams who did not make it far could have done so by showing a better performance, and I believe they failed to do this because of one of the following two common reasons:

1) <u>Fear.</u> When a team is facing a tough challenge - in the case of World Cup it will be facing one of the elite teams - sometimes fear dominates them, which affects their performance enormously and forces them to make mistakes. For example, it must be a very frightening experience for a modest team to face a team like Brazil, but if the players go to the field with a strong fighting morale and without any

fear, they will have a decent chance to beat even Brazil.

2) <u>Acceptance.</u> This is also called lack of motivation or building boundaries. The team in this case is happy to make it to World Cup and they strongly believe they have no chance to win or make it to the final. For the team, they have achieved the ultimate goal. They will play the games, but you can tell they do not believe deep inside they can go far and they do not put up a strong fight.
Of course, why would someone struggle if they know for a fact they were not going any further? This is where a strong team leader can shine and inspire the team, raising the bar for them beyond just the participation goal and fire them up to reach higher. It is not an easy process, and it takes a good amount of time to convince someone they can do more than what they think.

France

The French usually compete with a good team, and during this World Cup, it was no different. The team included some good names and world-class players. It may have not been the most favorite team to win the world cup, but everyone expected them to go far in the competition and show good results.

The problem was that the team lacked the main key factor and the most important foundation for any team. Trust.

The players did not trust each other. They were fighting and competing among themselves. They also did not have faith in the ability of their coach and refused to show up for training. This is the worst thing that can happen to a team. Anyone managing a team who finds themselves in a situation like this should stop everything and straighten the situation out before anything else and if there is no hope, replace the team and start over. It is better to do this than to be humiliated.

The French team with all its stars could not win one single game in the tournament. They played three games, tied in one game (0-0) and lost the other two games against Mexico and South Africa. With every bad result, the situation got worse and the players started blaming each other more for the loss. Like a snowball that kept growing faster and larger, it wiped out the whole team. It was the biggest humiliation for the French team in the history of the World Cup and they went home after round one.

Unfortunately, this situation happens often in many corporations. Large teams are usually divided into groups and appointed group leaders.

I have seen these groups forget they belong to the same team and become independent entities, competing between themselves. Their leaders also become jealous of each other.

Sometimes the situation becomes so bad, the group leaders start focusing on ensuring the other groups fail rather than focusing on making their own group succeed. All this happens because there is no trust among the leaders. They are hungry for position and think the other leaders are going to steal their promotion.

Arrogance and pride also play a role, especially when a person thinks he or she is more intelligent than the other people in the group and start talking down to everyone.

Trust is the heart of a team. Without it, the team cannot survive. Team members need to act and think as one and not compete destructively.

<u>Bottom Line:</u> If there is no trust between the team members, if arrogance reigns among them and they are fighting and blaming each other, do not proceed with anything until the situation is solved or the team is replaced. There is no other solution for this except an embarrassing failure.

Italy

Italy won the previous World Cup in 2006 and decided to participate in 2010 with the same team. The idea was that these players are mature, strong, have a lot of experience and did it before, so they can do it again. Right?

Wrong.

History of World Cup shows it is very rare that a team can win two competitions back to back and for many reasons. It is difficult to become a champion but it is harder to remain one.
Living off their past glory, they thought they would win again using the same resources and tactics, but they did not even make it out of the first round.
It is difficult to remain a champion because you do not have a clear goal once you reach the top, making it hard to stay focused. While you are trying to reach the top, you can tell where you are at any time. You can see your destination and have all the excitement, reason and dedication to reach your goal. You can clearly see the progress you are making. The initiative is usually with the teams who have their eyes on that top goal and are trying to reach it.
The Italian team lacked the dedication and purpose to win. They should have injected the team with some fresh blood, players who are eager to win the World Cup the first time. The team should also have sketched new plans and styles of play because everyone who watched Italy win knew this team's strengths and weaknesses. They also knew each player's style.
The team tied with Paraguay and New Zealand, the weakest teams in the tournament, and went to the last game

of their group knowing they had to win or they were out. There was too much pressure on the team and fear of failure in their hearts. The lack of dedication put a lot of stress on the team. Slovakia managed to defeat them (3-2) and send them out of the tournament. The team woke up after scoring the first goal and tried to work harder to produce a miracle, but it was too late.

It is the same story in business. If a team achieves a big accomplishment in a large project, it does not mean any similar future project will be a huge success automatically. Some projects might look similar, but each situation is different and presents new challenges. The key is to make the team aware of this at all time.

Four years had passed since the last world cup and Italy was trying to use the same tactics as the previous one. It is true these tactics helped them win the 2006 World Cup but things change a lot in four years. Teams need to remain up to date and enhance their methods and processes, because what worked several years ago may not work as well now and is sometimes completely useless.

There are plenty of examples of corporations that were number one in the world and either went backward or out of business due to no creativity or improvements. They thought they made it to the top and from there on everything would become easier. By the time they woke up from their dream, their competitors were already way ahead of them and they could not catch up.

I remember once when our team met with a well-known handheld computer manufacturer and were discussing future technologies. One person from our team mentioned that mobile phones seemed to be getting smarter, so maybe it would be a good idea to integrate a phone with their handheld device. This was in early 2000 before the era of smartphones began. The marketing manager of the company laughed derisively and said something along the lines of, "You will never see a phone that has a computer chip in it. Phones are used to make calls and communicate while handheld computers perform sophisticated tasks and manage your data. The average phone users would never want to learn how to use a handheld computer to make a phone call."

Well, guess what? This company was later sold and lost its identity, even though they had one of the most successful handheld devices at the time. Meanwhile, phones are getting smarter every day and people are enjoying them more and more.

This is just an example on how easily someone who reached the top can fall asleep and not wake up until it is too late.

Bottom Line: You cannot live off your past glory and assume following projects will happen automatically now that you have reached the top. It is important to praise your team but make sure you always find ways to keep them interested, engaged and dedicated.

England

England was expecting their team to win the tournament this time. They had a good team and they counted on Wayne Rooney, as one of the best players in the world, to make a big difference and help them win the World Cup.

The team played the first round with the USA, Slovenia and Algeria. One British magazine took the first letters of each of these countries and wrote on the front page: EASY (for England, Algeria, Slovenia and Yanks, meaning USA), but what was supposed to be easy turned into a nightmare.

The team started poorly and had a tie (1-1) with the USA team. Their goalkeeper made a big mistake that led to the USA team's goal.

England played against Algeria next and could not score a single goal. They finished the game at 0-0, although Algeria is not a very strong team in comparison to the other top teams.

England had to win the final game in their group to pass to the second round. They won (1-0) against Slovenia, which was playing for the first time in the World Cup, and they barely made it to the second round.

Wayne did not score one single goal in all three games and was disappointing.

England met with Germany in the second round, lost (4-1) and was sent out. This was an unexpected result for both the fans and experts, so what was wrong?

Two main mistakes lead to England's loss and failure:
1) England counted a lot on one player to make a big difference. Even if this player is strong, putting so much pressure and expectation on one person

usually ends up causing this person to perform poorly, no matter how good the player is. Before the World Cup, Wayne was on most of the sports magazines, advertisements and news, which raised the bar very high and put a lot of pressure on his shoulders.
2) England invented soccer but they won the tournament only one time in 1966 at home. The problem is using the same tactic and style of play for the past forty years. There are no new tactics, methods or creativity.

Teams cannot continue using same methods, processes and technologies forever. I am not saying to jump on and adopt any new thing that comes out immediately, but at the same time, do not rely only on the same thing forever.

A team should always learn and build new techniques and processes, but the key to success is not only to know them, but also to know when and where to use them.

When England met Germany, they were almost certain that they could beat them, but the German team played differently and was using a new style and new methods that surprised the English team. Germany was not the same classic Germany they played before and England remained the same old England with the same traditional style the German team knew very well. The final score was 4-1 in favor of Germany.

<u>*Bottom Line:*</u> *Teams should not put a lot of pressure and expectation on one member, even if he/she is the best. The team member's performance will drop considerably under pressure and may make the other team members either jealous or very dependent on this member.*

A team should continuously change, progress, enhance and update its methods, technologies and processes. The technologies or processes that were once the top of the line become outdated and obsolete quickly.

People sometime say: "If it is not broken, do not fix it." Even though it might still do the job, at what cost and what speed? If a team does not update their processes and technologies, their competitors will. They will outperform them, taking a large portion of their market share by producing faster, cheaper and better quality and may even put the team out of business, same as Germany did with England in the World Cup.

United States Of America

The USA team played in the Confederation Cup Tournament before the World Cup. This is a mini-World Cup tournament played one year before the World Cup, which includes countries that are champions of their continent. USA was champion of North America, Brazil was champion of South America and Spain was champion of Europe, etcetera.

In this tournament, USA played well and beat Spain, the number one ranked team in the world, and went to the finals against Brazil (ranked second). The USA team was ahead by two goals at half time, but Brazil made an amazing comeback and scored three goals in the second half to win (3-2).

Nevertheless, the USA team proved it is able to compete with the top ranked teams in the world.

When the drawing for the World Cup groups happened, it placed USA against England, Slovenia and Algeria. The USA team knew that while they may not win against England, theoretically they had two games against Slovenia and Algeria they should win easily, given their ranking and experience in comparison to the other two teams.

Unfortunately, the USA fell in the same trap as the Italians. They had a tie against England and before the first half ended against Slovenia, they were behind 0-2.

They were forced to use everything they had to tie against Slovenia and then again to win against Algeria. They were on their way out of the tournament until Landon Donavan scored a dramatic winning goal against Algeria in the last minute of extended time of the second half.

USA then went to the second round and lost against Ghana after an extended-time play.

Landon Donavan described what happened to the USA by saying, "We were naive."

This can happen to any team in any business. The team performs amazingly and accomplishes very challenging tasks and then finds itself in front of smaller project. Then what happens? It underestimates the work needed for the small project and starts taking it shallowly until it is too late. By then, the team will have to work harder and/or overtime to complete the project. As with the USA team, it might work a few times but not every time. When this happens, the team will fail to deliver.

Sometimes after working on a large, challenging task and accomplishing it, team members might not desire to work on a small project again. They will start to feel like it is beneath them or boring. I am sure it was not very exciting for the USA team to play Slovenia or Algeria after playing Spain, England and Brazil. Managers need to make sure the team understands there is no small or large project (figuratively speaking). A project is a project and it needs to be done, and each project is as important as any other project.

It is necessary to praise a team after an amazing achievement, but the team also needs to be ready to handle new responsibilities quickly, no matter how small they seem to be in comparison to the accomplished ones.

The situation with the USA team was very disappointing. Many Americans got excited about their team and started watching the tournament, even those who never watch soccer. People started gathering in public squares and pubs, even if it was not on the same large scale as gatherings in Europe or other countries yet.

I am sure if the USA team had won against Ghana, they would have gone on to play Uruguay, which would have been a tough game but definitely not impossible. The USA team had a good chance to make it to the semifinals and possibly win third place in the world for the first time ever.

What is sad about this is the USA team lost against Ghana in the 2010 World Cup and also in the 2006 World Cup. One would think a team would have learned from their mistake and not have lost against the same team twice, especially since Ghana is ranked below the USA, but that did not happen. The fear of another failure to the same team could have loomed over the USA players and affected their performance. It is not always easy to overcome a past failure when you have to deal with the same challenge again.

Sometimes it feels like the job is so simple it will happen by itself, without much hassle. Unfortunately, this situation has cost victories for many teams over past decades. I wish the USA team had learned from those past lessons. Falling into an "easy" group will not happen all the time.

<u>Bottom Line:</u> *Let the team celebrate great accomplishments, but make sure the team is ready to move on to new endeavors quickly. It is usually common to underestimate a small project right after accomplishing a more important one, so ensure the team does not fall into this trap. The smaller tasks and projects get overlooked the most because the level of focus will be less than when facing a larger challenge.*

Brazil

Brazil is always the most favorite team for winning the World Cup or any tournament they participate in. They have the most skilled players in any position, including the backup players.

Although the 2010 team was not one of the best Brazilian teams that participated in the World Cup, it was still one of the favorites.

The team usually starts slowly in the tournament then picks up speed with each game and this year it was no different.

Brazil won the group lead as expected and moved on to the second round where they played an astonishing game against Chile and won 3-0.

Brazil proved to everyone they are still the favorite after the Chilean game with a great show of force.

Quarterfinals did not go as expected for Brazil. They met with the Holland team who also plays well and was on a winning streak of twenty-two consecutive games.

Everyone expected an amazing match, and it was. Brazil could not have started any better and they scored one goal in the first half and were close to scoring another. They went to the half time with a leading score of 1-0.

In the second half, they started well until one player (ironically, the same player who was behind their goal in the first half) committed a mistake by blocking his goalkeeper's view and allowing Holland to tie the score 1-1.

Although Brazil players are amazingly professional and strong, they usually do not handle pressure very well. Only few minutes after the first goal, they were clearly lost and Holland scored again shortly after that.

A few minutes after this, Felipe Melo, the same Brazilian player who scored against his team, lost his temper and stepped on a Dutch player, resulting in a red card and removal from the game. The situation became very difficult for Brazil, being short by one player and one goal against a very strong team that was willing to do anything to win. They lost the game.

The main thing to be learned from this is a team can have top professionals and be doing great but it only takes one mistake by one team member to make the entire team fail.

I believe the Brazilian coach should have replaced this player after the second goal with another player. If one team member is falling apart under pressure while all the other members are doing great, he or she needs to be pulled back altogether, provided with help from someone strong or moved to another project if there is no alternative.

Any team member, even the best one, may not recover quickly after a big mistake. Each person reacts differently, but usually when someone makes a mistake that could cause the team to lose the whole project (goal, sale, etc.), they will have hard time staying focused especially if there is only a short time left.

The fear of being the one responsible for failure will haunt this person like an awful nightmare. When one team member commits such a mistake, the manager needs to help them overcome it, especially if it is not too late.

When team members are forced to switch to another task, they might be upset. If his happens, the manager needs to speak with them calmly in a constructive way and help them work on their self-control after the project succeeds.

Everyone makes mistakes and the best players in the world lose their tempers and become emotional after a mistake occurs.

Each team member is vital to the success of the project or task, so the team needs to be chosen wisely to ensure all team members fit well in the same culture and work in harmony. The manager should monitor their work performance, as well as their attitude, morale and level of stress, making sure everyone is moving forward together. A team member with low morale can also bring down the morale of the whole team little by little.

No matter how great the team is it will have weak points, both as individuals and a group. Finding weaknesses might take time and trigger some failures but it is important to figure them out. In the case of Brazil, it was an amazing team with the best players, but they did not manage the tough, unexpected situations well.

Many teams face this challenge. As long as the project is going according to the plan, life is good and everything is perfect, but when unexpected problems occur, several team members lose their focus and make mistakes.

This problem also happens a lot at the management level. Sometimes managers cannot control their tempers, emotions or nerves when things are not going well or seem to be falling apart and their typical solution for this is usually more micro-managing and harassing the team. They should fire up the team and give them confidence when things are not going well, and not demoralize them or make them feel guilty.

Bottom Line: *It is important to always remember these three main team rules:*
1) *No matter how amazing the team members are, they will make mistakes. No one is perfect.*
2) *The team will succeed only if ALL the team members succeed in their tasks. All it takes is the failure of one team member to take the whole team down with them.*
3) *The team will move as fast as the slowest member in it, and as strong as the weakest member.*

Argentina

Argentina's team had the best player in the world (Lionel Messi), and their coach (Diego Maradona) is one of the best players in the history of the game.

The team depended a lot on Messi. They made him an idol and portrayed him as the ultimate hero who would take down any team, the same way England did with Wayne Rooney.

Argentineans played well at the beginning of the tournament, until the quarterfinals when they met with Germany.

Diego Maradona with his unmatchable ego, refused to even appear before the game in a press conference next to the very young German player, Thomas Muller. Maradona called Muller a "ball boy" and insisted that he leave the press conference. The irony about this story is that Thomas Muller himself scored the first goal for Germany against Argentina in the game.

Argentina lost the game to Germany (4-0). Messi did not score anything in all the games that Argentina played. He did not do a thing against Germany and Maradona was humiliated.

Many times, teams hire a very skilled professional, thinking they will perform miracles and fix all the team's problems, only to find the situation becomes worse than before.

The story with Messi is similar to what happened with England and Rooney (see England team review). The difference between Argentina and England is England lost due to lack of creativity and improvement, while Argentina lost from the lack of self-confidence of players who were blinded by Messi's halo.

When a manager relies too much on the best performing team member and idolizes them, they will kill the ambition and dedication of the rest of the team. Other team members will become dependent on this member and even careless, thinking this person will fix any problem that might occur or mistake they may cause.

Other team members who would like to work hard and become successful grow jealous and feel all the credit will go to this person regardless of who did the job. Their ambition dies and they start working and caring less. It is important that appreciation and credit for success goes to all team members because each one contributed to the success, regardless of the level.

On the other hand, this person will fall under so much pressure with unrealistic expectations that he or she will start making more mistakes and become lost. This goes back to the same principle we mentioned before. No team member is more important than another. No team member can do it all alone. Each is needed to succeed.

I used to lead a team of developers and I always used my personal motto to remind the team that I rely on them. My motto is: *"I can do anything, but I cannot do everything."*

Everyone should believe there is nothing they cannot do in their field of expertise, but at the same time, they should know they cannot do everything by themselves in a realistic time frame.

If the Argentina players all thought of themselves as being Lionel Messi, I believe they would have gone much further.

I feel the Argentina players believed every attack or play had to go through Messi. I did not sense a strong team mindset in this game. What can Messi do when surrounded by two or three defenders? What can even a strong team leader do alone when faced with a large number of problems?

Getting back to the "ball boy" story, someone great and very experienced like Maradona tends to underestimate an entry-level person like Thomas Muller. This is another mistake businesses make occasionally, thinking they have more experience and skills then their competitors, especially if the competitors are new in the field. They underestimate them only to find out later that the competitors came up with new ideas and passed them.

Bottom Line: Even the best team player in the world cannot do everything alone. The whole team's dedication is needed to succeed. No one person should be under the spotlight, promoted as the sole star of the team. Not only will this demoralize the other members and make them less productive because they become so dependent on this member, but it also puts a lot of pressure on that team player and causes them to make more mistakes. The idea of a golden child in a team is very bad.

Ghana

Anyone who follows the World Cup and knows the teams might be surprised to see me talking about Ghana after speaking of Brazil and Argentina. The fact is, Ghana did well, made it to the quarterfinals and lost in a very dramatic match, so they deserve to be mentioned this far in the book.

There are several reasons why I wanted to mention Ghana, and those reasons apply to most teams in any type of business.

Ghana benefited from the fact that the World Cup was held in Africa, so they had a lot of support from the African fans and governments, which raised their morale and carried them far in the tournament.

Ghana players knew they probably could not win the World Cup. It is nearly impossible to beat all these strong teams, but this did not prevent them from fighting extremely hard and getting to the quarterfinals. In fact, they should have been in the semifinals.

It is good that a team knows its limitations because this is the only way they can work on improvement instead of being too overconfident and failing. The key is to make sure the team is constantly trying to improve and overcome some of their limitations. One way to do this is by giving the team full support, like the support that Ghana got in the World Cup.

To fire up the team members, the leaders need to motivate and speak to them. They must pinpoint their limitations as an "area with the opportunity to improve" and not in a negative way.

Not all team members will have the same weaknesses and strength, so mix and match between one or more team members whose skills complete each other. This is a good way to help them learn, increase the level of trust between them and help them share their knowledge without feeling punished or incompetent.

Ghana should have won the game against Uruguay and passed to the semifinals, but what happened was tragic. In the last minute of extended time, the two teams were tied (1-1) and the ball was on its way to the inside of the Uruguay goal when the Uruguay player, Suarez, stopped the ball with his hand right at the goal line like a goal keeper. (If you are not familiar with this game, only the goalkeeper is allowed to use his arms or hands.) He was fired and Ghana was granted a penalty kick. A player's chance to score from a penalty kick is approximately seventy or eighty percent, so imagine the pressure on the player who is trying to shoot this penalty in the last minute, knowing all the hard work and everything the team accomplished so far depends on him.

No player or team member would want to be in that situation. It is very nerve-wracking. The best football players in the world have missed critical penalties under pressure. Unfortunately, Ghana did not have a strong, experienced player with nerves of steel to do this. Their chosen player missed, they went into extra time without scoring and had to perform another penalty shootout.

They ultimately lost to Uruguay.

The worst thing that can happen to a team is to get into a situation where everything relies on one team member and there is little time left. No team member wants to be the last one to finish his or her tasks or take on a last minute, critical task where the rest of the team can do nothing to help. If this happens, the team better have one or two elite members with strong experience and nerves of steel to handle such a situation. This is where experience is very important.

<u>Bottom Line</u>: The team should see its limitations as an opportunity for improvement. They should always have experienced team members and members with different skill-sets so they can learn from each other. A few elite team members should always be available to handle last minute critical situations.

The team should do everything to avoid getting into a situation where all the pressure and stress falls on one person's shoulders with very little time left.

Uruguay

If you follow World Cup regularly, but you haven't seen this World Cup, you might be surprised to see me also talking about the Uruguay team at this stage, but you will understand why momentarily.

We talked about micro-managing and dominating leaders forcing their methods on the team and how this affects some teams negatively. In the case of Uruguay, the situation was different.

I am sure the Uruguay team was hoping for good results, but maybe not expecting to rank number four in the tournament, making it all the way to semifinals.

Sometimes a special leader emerges in a team. One who knows how to motivate the team, lead by example and make the team go that extra mile. This is what happened with Uruguay and this leader was Diego Forlan.

Diego was not only the best player and leader in the Uruguay team, he was also elected the best player of the tournament and won the Golden Ball Trophy.

The Uruguay team did not rely on Forlan exclusively. They all fought and played hard, but they needed inspiration and Diego gave them this and more. Whenever the situation was looking bad, Diego was there to turn the tables around and put the team back in the game.

It is crucial for a team to have a strong leader who can make things happen by stepping up, doing what it takes to get the job done, raise the team's morale in hard times and make the impossible, possible.

It is not easy to find a "Diego Forlan" for every team, but they should keep looking. Sometimes they do not have to look very far. Given the right opportunities, it might be surprising to find some team members have these qualities, but need someone to show or guide them.

The ideal person for this position is someone who is capable to lead in whom the team has faith and can rely but not depend on (big difference here). This person needs to have nerves of steel and the ability to make a difference in the toughest situations. Finally, this person must lead by example. He or she will work with the team and do more than simply give orders and check status updates.

Both Ghana and Uruguay had tough times and things looked pretty bad for them during a few games. Time is the worst enemy of a team. It becomes very difficult close to the final whistle or deadline if the team is still missing opportunities to 'score' or is falling behind on their tasks.

For example, the effect of the Ghana player missing the critical penalty at the end of the game did not only affect him, it affected the whole team. The players probably started thinking about the possibility of failure and "bad luck". There was obvious fear and loss of communication and focus. Everything began to fall apart quickly. This is when a strong leader is most needed to bring them back together, inspire, fire up the team, reestablish communication and work with them side by side to get things done. Ghana did not have a leader like this, but Uruguay did and it helped them a lot in the most critical moments.

Anyone can be a leader, but not everyone can be a great leader.

Bottom Line: *It is important to have a strong leader for the team, someone who can step up and lead by example, especially in difficult situations, a team leader who can lift the team up, who can inspire everyone around. The team needs to be able to rely on the leader when needed without depending on his or her solely.*

Germany

We are down to the last three teams, those who finished in the first three places and for good reasons.

Diego Forlan was possibly the most amazing player in the tournament but in my opinion, the German team was the most amazing team in the tournament.

Many German players were new to the world cup and never played in this tournament before, so they lacked experience in comparison to other teams. At the beginning of the competition, most of the critics said Germany would not go far.

Despite their lack of experience, they won third place because they were very organized, played as a real team and were confident, dedicated and creative.

Before the competition began, Germany had a strong, skilled captain who was influential and had played in both the 2002 and 2006 World Cups. Their captain suffered an injury before the tournament and could not play in this World Cup. Many critics thought this would have a negative impact on the team due to lack of experience.

Against all odds, the team performed better without their injured captain despite several players' lack of experience. So, what lead to this?

First, despite their captain being a strong leader, he also had a lot of influence on the team and became the center of focus in most plays. Without him, the team went "wild" and played a new style of fast football, with rapid counter attacks and a solid defense. This new style of play created many problems for the teams who played against Germany.

The loss of Germany's captain had another advantage to it as well. Since there was no strong, influential leader, all the players felt equal and played "at the same level". Sometimes this provides better results.

I remember long time ago my town had a local basketball team. Our team had a coach who also trained the second division team of the club he played for (he did not play for our club). One day, we had a big tournament and it just so happened that both teams ended up playing against each other. Since the coach could not manage both teams in the same game, he chose his club's team and our team had to play the match without him.

Against all odds, our team won without a coach, versus a team that was better than ours. Because there was no leader, the players were in constant communication and made decisions by themselves based on the course of the game. Our team made it to the semifinals and the coach returned to our team (since his team lost). Even with a coach that time, our team lost the game.

I am not saying that having a coach or a leader is a bad idea, definitely not. The point I am trying to make is the coach and leader can at times become a problem for the team. They may restrain and prevent them from improving. The leader can make a difference when things are not going well and the team is losing focus, but a good leader will let them unleash their skills and give them freedom to excel. In this case, the team will perform much better than when it is tightly controlled.

Leaders should not impose their opinions and limit the creativity of the team. They should pull the team up with them, create opportunities and help people grow, encouraging them to share their ideas and opinions, otherwise it is better to not have one at all.

Back to Germany in the World Cup. The second reason they excelled was also due to the new players. Germany normally participates with a mature, experienced team, and has been set in this style for several years, always playing football according to the "German school". This time, they had more young players than usual.

The good thing about fresh, young team members is they have a long future in front of them and want to excel so they give their all.

If I were to recruit team members, I would not hesitate to hire a few entry-level members, as long as they are smart, love the job and are passionate about it. I would give them freedom to excel (under guidance, of course). Another positive point about new team players is they are better able to think outside the box, bringing new ideas to the table. Experienced team players are typically set in their ways (except for a very few) and do not like to venture too far outside their natural environment.

One final point about the German team is that there was no competition between the players for scoring the most goals. In other words, there was no selfishness.

It is common to see team members eager for credit and trying to ensure no one else gets more than them.

Many famous players will attempt a shot at the goal when they know the chance to score is minimal, while their colleague is free and begging them to pass to him or her to score. Their ego, starvation for credit and jealousy prevents them from doing so.

Germany was different. Yes, they had their strikers, but many players scored and you could tell that no one player was selfishly trying to score the most goals. They did not care who scored as long as they won. I wish all teams were like this. It is amazing how often I see people who hate and distrust their teammate. Some even try to make them fail on purpose out of jealousy or greed.

I recommend watching the Germany games again, especially against Argentina and England. Look at how amazing this team was and how happy the players were. Pay attention to the strong level of trust between them and how much they supported each other. This is what a team should look like.

Germany played against England. Taking into account my previous points about England, they were stuck with the same old-fashioned tactics and plays while Germany changed their style to a modern fast play. When England met Germany, they thought they could beat them because they were familiar with the German style of play, but the new German style took them off guard and they lost (4-1). As I said before, a team must progress by keeping up with new technologies and processes. Their competitors most certainly will and in doing so, pass them by. Once the team realizes this, it is usually too late.

Bottom Line: Sometimes it is better to have entry level team members who are fresh, dedicated, creative and hard working rather than old-fashioned, experienced team members or micro-managing leaders. The team members should have some margin of freedom to excel and come up with fresh ideas, otherwise it will be a one-man team.

Holland

Holland came second in the World Cup, which is the furthest they went in their World Cup history.

Since they made it all the way to second place, it is obvious this team has many of the good features and qualities we mentioned previously.

Holland's team had an outstanding twenty-four international games without a loss by the time they made it to the finals, which is huge in football.

The team had a strong leader, Wesley Sneijder, who led by example and did not micro-manage.

Sneijder excelled against Brazil. When his team was lagging behind (0-1), stressed and scared of losing, he scored two goals, turned the tables and took his team with him to the finals.

This is a good example of how a great team leader performs and steps up when most needed. The team leader should be like Sneijder and let the team know they can count on him or her. Show they are right there in front, not sitting behind giving orders.

In the final game, Sneijder and his team were facing a very tough challenge.

Holland previous teams made it twice to the finals in 1974 and 1978 and lost both times. In 1998 they made it to semifinals and also lost.

You can imagine the stress and nervousness of the team. Since they had not made it to the finals in thirty-two years, they knew how hard it was to get that far. It was a one-time chance they could not afford to miss. All of Holland was watching this game and counting on these eleven players to make history. Talk about pressure!

Holland played well in the finals to a certain extent and had a couple of big opportunities to score (especially with Arjen Robben), but they missed them.

The pressure was so strong and the players were very nervous, which made them miss opportunities and make mistakes.

Holland put up a good fight despite some mistakes in the defense and fouls committed as a result of tension, and they manage to keep the score tied 0-0. Overtime in football is thirty minutes and the players were exhausted but they kept playing. In the twenty-fifth minute of the overtime, only five minutes before the end of the game, one player from Holland's defense committed a fatal mistake and allowed Spain to score.

It might seem harsh to lose due to one mistake by one player after thirty-two years of trying to reach the finals again. After two years of winning all the qualification games, winning all the World Cup games and fighting in the finals until the one hundred fifteenth minute. This is the beauty of the World Cup. That is why it is so hard to be the champion.

We often find ourselves as a team working hard and late to finish a difficult task. How many times do the long hours, stress and pressure cause us to make mistakes?

Many times, the winning team is the one that commits one less mistake. It is hard to remain focused and not lose sight of the goal when you are tired, stressed and nervous.

Despite the loss, Holland did a good job and got the second place. The pressure was simply too strong on them.

Another thing not in favor for Holland was the fact they got to the finals twice in the history of this competition and lost both times.

The fear of another failure was looming above their heads. It is a tough situation when a team has failed more than once in the same task and must try it one more time under the same conditions.

These past failures become similar to a curse for some players, who may become convinced they cannot go further. The press all over the world was talking about how Holland made it to the finals twice before and lost. They kept showing the old games, which certainly did not help the current players. It was obvious from Holland's number of fouls and physical play at the beginning of the game, they were scared of repeating the same failures. It is difficult for team leaders to make them forget past failures and focus on the present task.

<u>Bottom Line</u>: Stress and pressure cause teams to make strong mistakes. A strong leader can take the team far and high, but all it takes is one small mistake to end a long, successful journey. The team needs to be careful of previous failures. The leaders need to ensure the team members are not haunted by these past failures and keep them focused on the current task.

Spain

The Spanish team won this tournament and came ahead of all the other teams. If you look at the results of this team in comparison to others, you will find they scored very low. Most of the games Spain won ended in their favor with a score of (1–0).

I think Spain's team motto was, "We will get the job done. We do not care about doing it in a very impressive way, we just want to do it right."

This is a valid and realistic motto. After all, you want to achieve your goal. Some teams focus on winning by putting on a big, impressive show of force and end up losing many times because the focus shifts to the "show" instead of the goal and end result.

Anyone who watched the World Cup could tell Spain's players had their eyes on the result at all times. You could tell they were extremely focused on "not making a mistake" as much as "scoring and winning".

This is another important point teams sometimes miss. Do not focus only on the result, but be extra cautious, making sure you do not cause mistakes while getting there because as we saw before, one mistake can be fatal or create a lot of stress.

It is not wrong to be extra cautious like the Spanish team. As they say, "Measure twice and cut only once." It is good for a team to double check to be certain they did not miss anything, verify the work, test the product thoroughly, etcetera.

I have worked with many people who think that finishing the task is the main goal. They try to do it as quickly as possible, only to discover after it is done there were many items they forgot or overlooked. They end up missing the deadline trying to correct the problems.

The deadline will not change if you make a mistake. Now the team has to work harder to fix mistakes while also working on remaining tasks. This is similar to what happened two times with the USA team. They started the game and ended up behind by one or two goals. Instead of playing to win, they found themselves having to struggle a great deal to repair the mistakes and tie with the other team before they could even think of trying to win.

Spain's qualities included everything I mentioned earlier in regards to a good team. They had experience and passion. They did not have a micro-manager or care who got the credit. They focused on the result and were very cautious not to make mistakes.

The German team had similar qualities, except they had several first-timers. When they met with Spain, the experience of the Spanish players won against the lack of experience of the Germans. This was the only game where the German players were nervous and made mistakes, while the Spanish players were more confident and in control.

In a post-game interview, one of the German players said, "We were scared. If we did not get scared, we might have had a better chance."

This is where experience proves itself. If everything between two teams matches, but one team has more experienced members, the experienced team will outperform the other team.

Spain managed to impose their rhythm of play and their rules on every team they played against, and this paid off in the end for them.

Spain forced every team they played against to make mistakes. In the finals, Holland was very nervous and ended up having to play with one less player than Spain because he was sent off after double fouls.

If a team has a strong competitor, Spain's strategy might be very useful. Do everything right, focus on the result and be very careful not to make mistakes. Make your opponent nervous, forcing them to commit mistakes.

It takes a lot of focus, training, trust and hard work to get to this point. You cannot let your concentration level drop for one second. The Spanish players kept this in mind and won.

One last thing I liked about the Spanish team is they treated each competitor and game as a completely new, independent challenge. They did not underestimate any of the other teams. They did not let their victory against a strong team make them lose focus on the next game or become overconfident.

The team was not dependent on only one or two players. All the players were talented and each participated in both scoring and defending. This made it difficult for other teams to determine the key players and neutralize them. Any team member from Spain could step up and change the game.

<u>Bottom Line</u>: This is the summary of all the previous lessons. You need a well-organized, professional team that does not care who gets credit. Always focus on the result and make the least possible number of mistakes. The team needs to make sure they finish the job correctly and on time. They must focus on both goals equally, "on time" and "right". The team cannot sacrifice one for another.

Conclusion

There is so much to discover and learn during a career, and watching an event that requires strong teamwork like the World Cup is a good place to do so. You can enjoy the games, have fun and also learn from the teams' mistakes.

The things we learn from such an event can help any team in real life if they remember these principles and apply them.

For example, as spectators, we tend to misjudge some teams, thinking that if they do not have much experience or a glorious history, they will fail in front of a strong team. Then again, we saw small teams beat some of the strongest teams in the tournament many times.

The World Cup taught us we cannot assume that if we accomplish a large and difficult project, the next one is going to be a walk in the park, even if small. Each project has its own problems, situation and conditions, and all it takes is one small detail to be overlooked to fail. This is the case of the USA team who won against Spain in the Confederation Cup. They fell into a very easy group and barely made it out, just to fail against Ghana again.

The World Cup taught us that a strong team leader can make a big difference (as in the case of Uruguay) but also be a complete hindrance to the team as in the cases of Argentina and Germany.

We learned that new, fresh blood is very good for a team, especially if they love what they are doing and they have a lot of dedication, but not at the expense of experience. Experience is still very important and when things are tight, it makes a big difference (as in the case of Spain versus Germany).

We learned it is not necessarily true that if a team is made of the best people in their domain, everything will be perfect. Brazil was a good example of this.

We learned that hiring one of the best team members in their field and expecting them to perform miracles does not work. You cannot focus the spotlight on one person and make him or her an idol because the team will lose dedication and focus and will rely on this person too much.

There are many other points the World Cup teaches us and you probably know all of them but I believe "seeing" these things cause failure or success in real life examples may help you remember them better and put them into perspective.

Whether you are a team leader trying to find better ways to fire up the team, a business owner who is trying to put together a team and figure out the best candidate or a member of a team trying to assess your role and find ways to progress and excel, I hope you find this book beneficial in your journey.

About the Author

George Daoud is an information technology consultant, with more than twenty years of experience during which he has led and managed several software development teams.

George published many technical articles and training materials for private companies' engineers and teams and has used his experience and expertise to write this book.

www.ingramcontent.com/pod-product-compliance
Lightning Source LLC
Chambersburg PA
CBHW061519180526
45171CB00001B/256